pizza

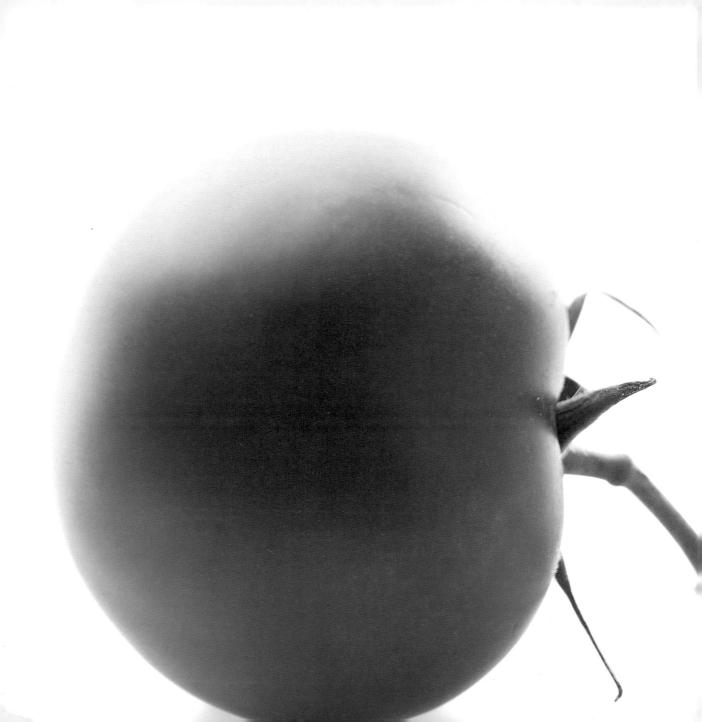

SILVANA FRANCO

pizza

photography by **William Lingwood**

RYLAND
PETERS
& SMALL
LONDON NEW YORK

First published in Great Britain in
2001 by Ryland Peters & Small
20–21 Jockey's Fields,
London WC1R 4BW
www.rylandpeters.com

This paperback edition first
published in 2006

Text, design and photographs
© Ryland Peters & Small 2001

10 9 8 7 6 5 4 3 2 1

ISBN 1 84597 074 8

A catalogue record for this book
is available from the British Library.

Printed and bound in China

Author's acknowledgements

Big thanks to my trusty side-kick
Annalisa Aldridge for her
enthusiastic recipe testing and
dough-kneading. Also to my best
friends and colleagues at Fork,
Angela and Jenny, who put up with
me day in, day out – thanks girls!
To my mum who fed me my first
ever slice of pizza. To the very
talented and patient William
Lingwood for the beautiful shots,
to Vanessa Davies for the portrait
and to all the team at Ryland
Peters & Small. And finally, to my
brand new husband Robert – just
remember, you're a very lucky man.

NOTES

All spoon measurements are level unless otherwise specified.
Fresh herbs are used in this book unless otherwise stated. If using dried
herbs, halve the quantity given.
Uncooked or partly cooked eggs should not be served to the very old
or frail, the very young or to pregnant women.
Ovens should be preheated to the specified temperature. Recipes in this
book were tested with a fan-assisted oven. If using a regular oven,
increase the cooking times according to the manufacturer's instructions.

Most of the recipes in this book call for a **pizza stone**, which is a thick,
unglazed ceramic slab. Preheated in the oven before the pizza is added,
it is the most reliable way of producing a perfect crisp but chewy crust.
Pizza stones are available in various sizes from all good cook shops.
Alternatively, use a preheated baking sheet.

Senior Designer
Paul Tilby

Commissioning Editor
Elsa Petersen-Schepelern

Editor
Sally Somers

Production
Patricia Harrington

Art Director
Gabriella Le Grazie

Publishing Director
Alison Starling

Food Stylist
Silvana Franco

Stylist
Liz Belton

Photographer's Assistant
Anna Bentham

contents

6 **INTRODUCTION**

8 **BASICS**

12 **CLASSIC PIZZA**

28 **VEGETARIAN PIZZA**

36 **SEAFOOD PIZZA**

42 **PIZZA** WITH **MEAT**

60 **SWEET PIZZA**

64 **INDEX**

introduction

I grew up in an Italian household, where pizza always played a key role at the family table. Every month, my mother would spend a whole day pounding dough and turning out oven-sized trays of classic Margherita and calzones. For about a week, we would all tuck into them at pretty well any time of day. While few of us have time to spend such long hours in the kitchen, my simple recipes for delicious homemade pizzas – enough just for two or four people – show you how easy and speedy it can be.

Once you have made a few pizzas, you'll find that you really get a feel for the texture of the dough, and will make the decision yourself as to the thickness and size of your bases. Soon, you'll find yourself being increasingly daring and inventive with your choice of toppings. Have fun, that's what cooking and eating pizza is all about!

I have only two really essential tips to share with you: firstly, don't skimp when it comes to kneading the dough. It has to have at least 10 minutes of good, vigorous pounding to bring out its elasticity. If you don't have the energy, or you want to make a big amount, invest in a large electric mixer with a dough hook. Secondly, never put pizza into a cold oven – it will come out dense and soggy rather than light and crispy.

Oh, and make sure you have plenty of good red wine or ice cold beer on hand!

basic pizza dough

For a really good pizza dough, try to use the superfine durum wheat '00' flour, which you can buy in Italian stores and large supermarkets. Otherwise, choose a strong white bread flour. Some cooks add flavourings such as chopped herbs or grated cheese to the dough, but I like to keep it simple and let the toppings take centre stage.

250 g tipo 00 or strong white bread flour, plus extra for sprinkling

½ teaspoon table salt

7 g sachet easyblend dried yeast

2 tablespoons olive oil

125 ml tepid water

MAKES 1 LARGE PIZZA BASE

Put the flour, salt and yeast in a large bowl and mix. Make a well in the centre. Add the oil and water to the well and gradually work in the flour to make a soft dough. Sprinkle over a little flour if the mixture feels too sticky, but make sure it is not too dry: the dough should be pliable and smooth.

Transfer the dough onto a lightly floured surface. Knead for 10 minutes, sprinkling with flour when needed, until the dough is smooth and stretchy.

Rub some oil over the surface of the dough and return the dough to the bowl. Cover with a clean tea towel and leave for about 1 hour, until the dough has doubled in size.

Remove the dough to a lightly floured surface and knead for 2 minutes, until the excess air is knocked out. Roll out the dough according to the recipe you are following.

POLENTA DOUGH

To make a polenta base, use 50 g fine polenta or cornmeal and 200 g strong white bread flour.

NOTE: *If you are in a real hurry, there are some good quality packet dough mixes available. Follow the instructions on the packet, but remember to roll it out to very thin.*

basics

classic tomato sauce

This simple sauce is perfect as a basic topping for almost any pizza. Choose cans of whole plum tomatoes rather than the chopped sort, which can have a bitter edge. Remember to cook the sauce for at least thirty minutes to give it time to develop some richness.

Heat the oil in a small saucepan, add the shallot and garlic and cook for 3–4 minutes until softened. Add the tomatoes, breaking them up briefly with a wooden spoon. Add the herbs, sugar, and salt and pepper to taste.

Bring to the boil and part cover with the lid. Reduce the heat and simmer very gently for 30–60 minutes, stirring from time to time and breaking the tomatoes down with the back of the spoon, until the sauce turns a dark red and droplets of oil appear on the surface.

Discard any woody herb sprigs. Taste and adjust the seasoning, then let cool slightly before using.

1 tablespoon olive oil

1 shallot, finely chopped

2 garlic cloves, finely chopped

400 g canned whole plum tomatoes

a sprig of fresh rosemary or thyme, or a pinch of dried oregano

a pinch of sugar

sea salt and freshly ground black pepper

MAKES ENOUGH FOR 1 LARGE PIZZA

fiery tomato sauce

The crushed dried chillies add an extra kick to this smooth, satiny sauce. Use it as an alternative to the classic tomato sauce in any of these pizza recipes. The basil is not essential, but is worth adding if you have some to hand.

500 g carton creamed tomatoes or passata

2 tablespoons olive oil

2 garlic cloves, finely chopped

6 basil leaves, torn

a pinch of crushed dried chillies

$\frac{1}{4}$ teaspoon sugar

sea salt and freshly ground black pepper

MAKES ENOUGH FOR
1 LARGE PIZZA

Put the tomatoes, oil, garlic, basil, chillies and sugar in a saucepan with salt and pepper to taste.

Bring to the boil and part cover with a lid. Reduce the heat and simmer very gently, stirring from time to time, for 30–60 minutes, until the sauce turns a dark red and droplets of oil appear on the surface.

Taste and adjust the seasoning, cover with the lid and let cool slightly before using.

The secret to a delicious Marinara is in the tomatoes. Choose really ripe, plump varieties. It's well worth the extra effort of skinning and deseeding them – the result is a satin-smooth, fragrant and fruity sauce. Don't be tempted to add any cheese!

marinara

Put a pizza stone or baking sheet in the oven and preheat the oven to 220°C (425°F) Gas 7.

Heat 2 tablespoons of the oil in a saucepan and add the tomatoes and salt and pepper to taste. Cook for about 5 minutes, stirring occasionally, until thickened and pulpy.

Roll out the dough on a lightly floured surface to 30 cm diameter and brush with a little oil. Spoon over the tomato sauce and scatter evenly with the garlic and oregano or marjoram. Drizzle with a little more oil.

Transfer the pizza to the hot pizza stone or baking sheet and cook for 15–20 minutes, until crisp and golden.

3–4 tablespoons olive oil

700 g ripe tomatoes, skinned, deseeded and diced

1 recipe pizza dough (page 8)

3 garlic cloves, very thinly sliced

1 tablespoon chopped fresh oregano or marjoram

sea salt and freshly ground black pepper

MAKES 1

classic pizza

margherita

The red, white and green on this pizza – named after the queen of Italy to honour her visit to Naples just over a century ago – symbolize the *tricolore* of the Italian flag. Since the topping is so simple, try to use the best ingredients you can find, such as imported Italian buffalo mozzarella.

1 recipe pizza dough (page 8)

2 tablespoons olive oil

1 recipe tomato sauce (page 10)

200 g small tomatoes, quartered or sliced

150 g mozzarella cheese, drained and sliced

sea salt and freshly ground black pepper

a handful of fresh basil leaves

MAKES 1

Put a pizza stone or baking sheet in the oven and preheat the oven to 200°C (400°F) Gas 6.

Roll out the dough on a lightly floured surface to 30 cm diameter and brush with half the oil. Spoon over the tomato sauce and arrange the tomatoes and mozzarella on top.

Drizzle the pizza with the remaining oil and sprinkle with salt and plenty of black pepper. Carefully transfer to the hot pizza stone or baking sheet and cook for 20–25 minutes, until crisp and golden.

Scatter the basil leaves over the hot pizza. Cut into wedges and serve.

2 red peppers

2 yellow peppers

2 garlic cloves, finely chopped

a small bunch of flat leaf parsley, finely chopped

2 tablespoons olive oil

1 recipe pizza dough (page 8)

1 recipe tomato sauce (pages 10–11)

150 g tomatoes, sliced or halved

150 g mozzarella cheese, drained and sliced

sea salt and freshly ground black pepper

MAKES 1

Put a pizza stone or baking sheet in the oven and preheat the oven to 220°C (425°F) Gas 7. Put the peppers in a small roasting tin and bake for 30 minutes, turning them occasionally, until the skin blisters and blackens.

Meanwhile, put the garlic and parsley in a bowl. Add the oil and salt and pepper to taste.

Remove the peppers from the oven, cover with a clean tea towel and set aside for about 10 minutes, until cool enough to handle but still warm. Pierce the bottom of each pepper and squeeze the juices into the parsley and oil mixture. Skin and deseed the peppers. Cut the flesh into 2 cm strips and add to the mixture. Cover and set aside at room temperature until needed.

Roll out the dough on a lightly floured surface to 30 cm diameter and brush with a little oil. Spoon over the tomato sauce and arrange the tomatoes and mozzarella on top. Spoon the pepper mixture over the top.

Carefully transfer to the hot pizza stone or baking sheet and cook for 20–25 minutes, until crisp and golden. Cut into wedges and serve.

roasted pepper pizza

Roasting peppers is a lovely way to bring out their sweetness. Make sure the peppers are still warm when you add the flesh to the dressing, so that they absorb the flavours of the garlic and parsley.

mushroom with basil, chilli and garlic oil

Mushrooms are always an excellent choice for pizza toppings. For a range of flavour and texture I like to use a mixture of varieties, including chestnut, shiitake and field. The basil, chilli and garlic oil isn't essential, but adds quite a boost. Some food stores stock infused oils, such as basil or lemon oil, which would make a good substitute.

Put a pizza stone or baking sheet in the oven and preheat the oven to 220°C (425°F) Gas 7.

Roll out the dough on a lightly floured surface to 30 cm diameter and brush with a little oil. Spoon over the tomato sauce and scatter over the mushrooms and mozzarella.

Drizzle the pizza with a little oil and sprinkle with salt and pepper. Carefully transfer to the hot pizza stone or baking sheet and cook for 20–25 minutes, until crisp and golden.

Meanwhile, put the remaining oil in a small saucepan with the garlic and chilli. Heat very gently for 10 minutes, until the garlic is softened and translucent. Remove from the heat and set aside to cool slightly for 5 minutes.

Using a fork, remove and discard the garlic and chilli. Stir the basil into the flavoured oil and drizzle over the hot pizza. Cut into wedges and serve.

1 recipe pizza dough (page 8)

8 tablespoons olive oil

1 recipe tomato sauce (pages 10–11)

400 g mixed mushrooms, thickly sliced

150 g mozzarella cheese, drained and diced

2 plump garlic cloves, halved

1 large, mild red chilli, deseeded and quartered

8 fresh basil leaves, finely shredded

sea salt and freshly ground black pepper

MAKES 1

aubergine with bresaola, rocket and parmesan

Bresaola, dried lean beef from the Alpine region of Italy, has a lovely sweetness which here complements the peppery rocket and salty Parmesan. If you can't find bresaola, use a dry-cure ham, such as serrano or prosciutto.

1 aubergine, cut into 1 cm rounds

3–4 tablespoons olive oil, plus extra to serve

1 recipe pizza dough (page 8)

1 recipe tomato sauce (pages 10–11)

100 g very thinly sliced bresaola or cured ham

50 g fresh rocket leaves

Parmesan cheese, freshly grated or shaved

sea salt and freshly ground black pepper

MAKES 1

Put a pizza stone or baking sheet in the oven and preheat the oven to 200°C (400°F) Gas 6. Brush the aubergine slices with the oil and sprinkle salt and pepper lightly on both sides. Preheat a stove-top grill pan, add the aubergines and cook for 3–4 minutes on each side, until tender and browned.

Roll out the dough on a lightly floured surface to 30 cm diameter and brush with a little oil. Spoon over the tomato sauce and arrange the aubergine slices on top.

Transfer to the hot pizza stone or baking sheet and cook for 15 minutes. Remove from the oven and ripple the bresaola or ham evenly across the pizza. Return the pizza to the oven and cook for a further 5–10 minutes, until crisp and golden.

Sprinkle with the rocket leaves and Parmesan. Top with a splash of olive oil and a good grinding of black pepper. Cut into wedges and serve.

4 tablespoons olive oil

1 shallot, thinly sliced

150 g chestnut
mushrooms, sliced

2 tablespoons chopped
fresh parsley

1 recipe pizza dough
(page 8)

1 recipe tomato sauce
(pages 10–11)

50 g Parma ham,
shredded

6 black olives

4 artichoke hearts in
brine or oil, drained and
quartered

75 g mozzarella cheese,
drained and sliced

4 anchovy fillets in oil,
drained

sea salt and freshly
ground black pepper

basil leaves, to serve

MAKES 1

quattro stagioni

The pizza for those who just can't make up their minds which one they want. You get all the best bits at once with this one.

Put a pizza stone or baking sheet in the oven and preheat the oven to 200°C (400°F) Gas 6.

Heat 2 tablespoons of the oil in a frying pan and cook the shallot for 2 minutes. Add the mushrooms and cook for a further 2–3 minutes, until softened and golden. Stir in the parsley and add salt and pepper to taste.

Roll out the dough on a lightly floured surface to 30 cm diameter and brush with a little oil. Spoon over the tomato sauce.

Pile the mushrooms over one quarter of the pizza. Arrange the ham and olives on another quarter and the artichoke hearts on the third section of pizza. Lay the mozzarella on the remaining section and put the anchovies on top.

Drizzle a little more oil over the whole pizza and sprinkle with salt and plenty of black pepper. Carefully transfer to the hot pizza stone or baking sheet and cook for 20–25 minutes, until crisp and golden. Cut into quarters, sprinkle the basil over the artichoke portion and serve.

A super-thick pizza with a deep crust you can really sink your teeth into. To be sure of a crisp base, I cook this in a proper pizza pan, which has holes in the bottom to allow the steam to escape.

chicago deep pan pepperoni

double recipe pizza dough (page 8)

2 tablespoons olive oil

½ recipe tomato sauce (pages 10–11)

1 large tomato, sliced

1 small red onion, sliced and separated into rings

150 g mozzarella cheese, drained and sliced

100 g sliced pepperoni

sea salt and freshly ground black pepper

MAKES 1

Preheat the oven to 200°C (400°F) Gas 6.

Roll out the dough on a lightly floured surface to 30 cm diameter and push into a pizza pan or put onto a pizza stone or baking sheet. Brush with 1 tablespoon of the oil and spoon over the tomato sauce.

Arrange the tomato slices over the sauce. Lay the onion rings on top, splash over the remaining oil and sprinkle with salt and plenty of black pepper. Put into the preheated oven and cook for 20 minutes.

Remove from the oven and arrange the mozzarella and pepperoni slices over the top. Return the pizza to the oven and cook for a further 10–15 minutes, until risen and golden. Cut into wedges and serve.

There isn't much to beat warm, freshly baked focaccia. The key to the lovely, soft texture is to cover the bread with a tea towel as soon as it comes out of the oven – the steam will prevent a hard crust from forming. You can vary the ingredients by adding chopped olives, tiny cubes of cheese or chopped fresh thyme. Focaccia is best eaten within a day or two of making.

tomato focaccia

500 g tipo 00 or strong
white bread flour

1 teaspoon table salt

7 g sachet
easyblend dried yeast

3 tablespoons olive oil

6 sun-dried tomatoes in
oil, drained and chopped

275 ml tepid water

1 teaspoon coarse
sea salt

a sprig of rosemary,
chopped

2 tablespoons chilli oil

SERVES 6

Put the flour, table salt and yeast in a large bowl and mix. Make a well in the centre. Add 2 tablespoons of the olive oil, the sun-dried tomatoes and water to the well, then gradually work in the flour to make a soft dough. Sprinkle over a little flour if the mixture feels too sticky, but make sure it's not dry. The dough should be pliable and smooth.

Transfer the dough onto a lightly floured surface and knead for 10 minutes, sprinkling with flour when needed, until the dough is smooth and stretchy.

Rub some oil over the surface and return the dough to the bowl. Cover with a tea towel and leave for about 1 hour, until the mixture has doubled in size.

Remove the dough to a lightly floured surface and knead for 2 minutes, until the excess air is knocked out. Roll out the dough to make an oval, about 32 cm long. Carefully transfer to a baking sheet and cover with a clean tea towel. Set aside for 30 minutes until almost doubled in size. Meanwhile, preheat the oven to 200°C (400°F) Gas 6.

Using your fingertips, make indents about 2 cm deep into the surface of the risen dough. Drizzle with the remaining olive oil and sprinkle with the sea salt and rosemary. Bake for 20–25 minutes, until risen and golden.

Remove the focaccia from the oven, cover with a tea towel and set aside for at least 15 minutes to cool. Drizzle with the chilli oil. Serve warm or at room temperature.

vegetarian pizza

wafer potato pizza with taleggio

A light and crispy pizza with a delicate flavour. Serve for a summery lunch with a tomato and red onion salad.

1 recipe pizza dough (page 8)

2 tablespoons olive oil

350 g red-skinned potatoes

6 sage leaves, finely shredded

2 garlic cloves, crushed

200 g Taleggio cheese, diced

sea salt and freshly ground black pepper

MAKES 4

Put a pizza stone or baking sheet in the oven and preheat the oven to 200°C (400°F) Gas 6.

Divide the dough into 4 and, on a lightly floured surface, roll each piece into a wafer-thin oval, about 28 cm long. Brush the dough ovals with 1 tablespoon of the oil.

Using a mandoline or food processor, cut the potatoes into wafer-thin slices. Put the slices into a bowl, add the sage, garlic and remaining tablespoon of oil and toss to coat. Put a single layer of potato slices over each dough base and sprinkle with salt and plenty of black pepper.

Carefully transfer to the hot pizza stone or baking sheet and cook for 10 minutes. Remove from the oven and scatter over the Taleggio. Return the pizza to the oven and cook for a further 5–10 minutes, until crisp and golden. Serve hot or warm.

charred vegetable polenta pizza

A robust pizza packed with flavour. Eat this straight from the oven, while the cheese is still bubbling.

Put a pizza stone or baking sheet in the oven and preheat the oven to 220°C (425°F) Gas 7.

Put the courgette, aubergine, tomatoes, garlic, red onion and thyme in a roasting tin. Add salt and pepper and drizzle with the oil. Cook for 30 minutes, stirring from time to time, until softened and a little charred.

Lower the oven temperature to 200°C (400°F) Gas 6. Roll out the dough on a lightly floured surface to 30 cm diameter and spoon the vegetables over the top.

Carefully transfer the dough to the hot pizza stone or baking sheet and cook for 15 minutes. Remove from the oven and top with the dolcelatte. Return the pizza to the oven and cook for a further 5–10 minutes, until crisp and golden.

Sprinkle with the basil leaves, cut into wedges and serve hot.

1 courgette, thickly sliced

1 small aubergine, cubed

4 plum tomatoes, halved

8 unpeeled garlic cloves

1 red onion, cut into wedges

a few sprigs of thyme

2 tablespoons olive oil

1 recipe polenta pizza dough (page 8)

150 g dolcelatte cheese, diced

sea salt and freshly ground black pepper

a handful of fresh basil leaves, to serve

MAKES 1

molten cheese and gremolata calzone

The herby, zingy gremolata is wonderful with the creamy melted cheese. This is an impressive little number which always goes down a storm.

Put a pizza stone or baking sheet in the oven and preheat the oven to 200°C (400°F) Gas 6.

To make the gremolata, put the garlic, parsley, lemon zest, oil and salt and pepper in a bowl and mix well.

Divide the dough into 6. Put on a lightly floured surface and roll each piece into an oval about 25 cm long. Cut the cheese into 6 even slices or wedges and put a slice on one half of each dough oval. Spoon the gremolata over the cheese. Dampen the edges of the dough and fold the dough over to enclose the filling. Press the edges together firmly to seal.

Transfer to the hot pizza stone or baking sheet, dust with a little flour and bake for 20–25 minutes, until crisp and golden. Serve hot.

2 garlic cloves, crushed

15 g flat leaf parsley, finely chopped

grated zest of 1 lemon

1 tablespoon olive oil

400 g Taleggio, Brie or Camembert cheese

double recipe pizza dough (page 8)

flour, for dusting

sea salt and freshly ground black pepper

MAKES 6

fiorentina

Spinach and egg pizzas are a favourite in pizza restaurants everywhere, and you can easily make them at home. It doesn't matter if the yolk is a bit hard, but make sure it goes onto the pizza whole.

350 g young spinach leaves

1 tablespoon butter

2 garlic cloves, crushed

1 recipe pizza dough (page 8)

1–2 tablespoons olive oil

1 recipe tomato sauce (pages 10–11)

150 g mozzarella cheese, drained and thinly sliced

4 small eggs

50 g fontina or Gruyère cheese, finely grated

sea salt and freshly ground black pepper

MAKES 1

Put a pizza stone or baking sheet in the oven and preheat the oven to 220°C (425°F) Gas 7.

Wash the spinach thoroughly and put into a large saucepan. Cover with a lid and cook for 2–3 minutes, until the spinach wilts. Drain well and, when the spinach is cool enough to handle, squeeze out any excess water with your hands.

Melt the butter in a frying pan and cook the garlic for 1 minute. Add the drained spinach and cook for a further 3–4 minutes. Add salt and pepper to taste.

Divide the dough into 4, put on a lightly floured surface and roll out each piece to about 17 cm diameter. Brush with a little oil and spoon over the tomato sauce. Put the spinach on the bases, leaving a space in the middle for the egg. Put the mozzarella on top of the spinach, drizzle with a little more oil and sprinkle with salt and plenty of black pepper.

Carefully transfer to the hot pizza stone or baking sheet and cook for 10 minutes. Remove from the oven and crack an egg into the middle of each pizza. Top with the fontina or Gruyère and return to the oven for a further 5–10 minutes, until the base is crisp and golden and the eggs have just set. Serve immediately.

anchovy butter and mozzarella

My favourite pizza – it always delights me that something this simple can be so loaded with flavour. I keep a roll of the anchovy butter in my freezer, so I can cut slices from the frozen roll to toss with baby new potatoes or pasta.

4 anchovy fillets in oil, drained

2 garlic cloves

2 tablespoons coarsely chopped flat leaf parsley

1 tablespoon drained capers

50 g unsalted butter, at room temperature

1 recipe pizza dough (page 8)

150 g mozzarella cheese, drained and sliced

freshly ground black pepper

MAKES 1

Put a pizza stone or baking sheet in the oven and preheat the oven to 200°C (400°F) Gas 6.

Put the anchovies, garlic, parsley and capers in a food processor and pulse until finely chopped. Remove the mixture to a bowl and add the butter. Mix well, adding plenty of black pepper. Cover and refrigerate.

Roll out the dough on a lightly floured surface to about 30 cm diameter and prick all over with a fork. Transfer to the hot pizza stone or baking sheet and cook for 15 minutes.

Remove from the oven and arrange the mozzarella over the pizza. Dot with teaspoons of the anchovy butter and return to the oven for a further 5–10 minutes, until the pizza is crisp and golden. Cut into wedges and serve.

seafood pizza

Put a pizza stone or baking sheet in the oven and preheat the oven to 200°C (400°F) Gas 6.

Wash the mussels thoroughly, removing the beards and discarding any with broken shells. Put into a large saucepan and cover with a tightly fitting lid. Cook over a high heat for 3–4 minutes, shaking the pan from time to time, until the shells open. Drain well, let cool, then remove the mussels from their shells. Discard the empty shells and any that have not opened.

For the pesto, put the basil, mint, garlic, chilli, lemon zest, pistachios and Parmesan in a blender or food processor. Pulse until blended. Add the oil, some salt and plenty of black pepper and blend to a smooth paste.

Divide the dough into 6, put on a lightly floured surface and roll out each piece to about 12 cm diameter. Brush each round with oil and prick all over with a fork. Transfer to the hot pizza stone or baking sheet and cook for 10–12 minutes.

Remove from the oven and divide the shelled mussels among the pizzette rounds. Drizzle over the pesto and return to the oven for 3–4 minutes more, until crisp and golden. Sprinkle with Parmesan and serve warm.

500 g mussels in shells

25 g fresh basil leaves

10 fresh mint leaves

1 garlic clove

1 small red chilli, deseeded and coarsely chopped

grated zest of ½ lemon

1 tablespoon shelled pistachios

2 tablespoons freshly grated Parmesan cheese, plus extra to serve

6 tablespoons olive oil

1 recipe pizza dough (page 8)

sea salt and freshly ground black pepper

MAKES 6

mussel and pesto pizzette

Pizzette means 'little pizzas', and these can be downscaled even further into bite-sized canapés, each with a single mussel on top. The pesto can be used in all sorts of other dishes – try stirring it into creamy mashed potatoes or risotto.

I love putting prawns on a pizza and, although
they don't go well with other kinds of cheese,
I find they're fantastic with creamy mascarpone.
I always use the fiery tomato sauce for this one.

prawn and
sun-dried tomato

1 recipe pizza dough (page 8)

2 tablespoons olive oil

1 recipe fiery tomato sauce (page 11)

100 g semi-dried tomatoes, such as the 'sun-blushed' variety

100 g mascarpone cheese

250 g large, cooked, peeled prawns

sea salt and freshly ground black pepper

6 spring onions, finely shredded, to serve

MAKES 1

Put a pizza stone or baking sheet in the oven and preheat the oven to 200°C (400°F) Gas 6.

Roll out the dough on a lightly floured surface to 30 cm diameter and brush with 1 tablespoon of the oil. Spoon over the tomato sauce and scatter the tomatoes on top.

Drizzle the pizza with the remaining oil. Sprinkle with salt and plenty of black pepper. Carefully transfer to the hot pizza stone or baking sheet and cook for 15 minutes.

Remove from the oven and spoon small dollops of mascarpone over the pizza. Top with the prawns and return to the oven for a further 5–10 minutes, until crisp and golden. Scatter with the spring onions, cut into wedges and serve.

pizza with meat

parma and fontina pizza sandwich

Sliced into long fingers or triangles and served with a simple salad, this pizza makes an elegant starter. Alternatively, cut it into smaller pieces to serve warm with pre-dinner drinks.

1 recipe pizza dough (page 8)

100 g Parma ham

200 g fontina cheese, finely grated

35 g fresh rocket leaves

2 tablespoons olive oil

freshly ground black pepper

SERVES 4

Put a pizza stone or baking sheet in the oven and preheat the oven to 200°C (400°F) Gas 6.

Divide the dough in half, put on a lightly floured surface and roll each half into a 25 cm square.

Layer the Parma ham on one of the squares, leaving a 1 cm border all round. Scatter the fontina evenly over the top. Top with rocket leaves and sprinkle with black pepper.

Dampen the border with a little water and put the second square of dough on top. Press the edges firmly together to seal.

Drizzle with oil and transfer to the hot pizza stone or baking sheet. Cook for 20–25 minutes, until crisp and golden. Cut into squares, fingers or triangles and serve warm.

english breakfast pizza

All the best bits of a good English breakfast are right here on a pizza. The portions are hearty, so make sure you have worked up a really good appetite before you start.

Put 2 pizza stones or baking sheets in the oven and preheat the oven to 200°C (400°F) Gas 6. Divide the dough in half, put on a lightly floured surface and roll out each half to 20 cm diameter. Spread the mustard and ketchup over each base. Arrange the tomatoes, sausages, bacon and mushrooms on each pizza, leaving a space in the middle for the egg.

Drizzle with a little oil and carefully transfer to the hot pizza stones or baking sheets. Cook for 15 minutes, then remove from the oven and increase the temperature to 220°C (425°F) Gas 7.

Crack an egg into the middle of each pizza and sprinkle with salt and pepper. Return the pizzas to the oven and cook for a further 5–10 minutes, until the egg is just set and the base is crisp and golden. Scatter over the chopped parsley and serve warm.

1 recipe pizza dough
(page 8)

2 teaspoons wholegrain
mustard

2 teaspoons tomato
ketchup

5 small tomatoes, halved
crossways

6 pork chipolata
sausages

6 slices smoked streaky
bacon

5 chestnut mushrooms,
halved

2 eggs

1 tablespoon olive oil

sea salt and freshly
ground black pepper

1 tablespoon chopped
fresh parsley, to serve

MAKES 1

topsy turvy cherry tomato pizza

Cooking a pizza upside down is a great way to make sure you get a crisp crust. It also keeps all the lovely tomato juices from escaping – the result is spectacular.

2–3 tablespoons olive oil

100 g pancetta or unsmoked streaky bacon, cut into cubes

1.2 kg cherry tomatoes

1 recipe pizza dough (page 8)

juice of 1 lime

2 teaspoons chopped fresh mint

sea salt and freshly ground black pepper

Swiss roll tin or baking tray, about 35 x 25 cm

MAKES 1

Preheat the oven to 200°C (400°F) Gas 6.

Heat 1 tablespoon of the oil in a large frying pan and cook the pancetta or bacon cubes for 2–3 minutes, until golden.

Transfer the pancetta or bacon and the pan oil to the Swiss roll tin or baking tray. Put the cherry tomatoes in the tin, making sure that they fit in a single layer. Sprinkle with salt and pepper.

Roll out the dough on a lightly floured surface to about the same size as the tin. Put the dough on top of the tomatoes, tucking any overlap inside the tin. Bake for 20–25 minutes, until the crust is crisp and dark golden.

Meanwhile, mix the lime juice, mint and remaining oil in a bowl.

Carefully invert the pizza onto a chopping board. Drizzle the lime and mint mixture over the top. Slice and serve warm.

potato dough pizza
with salami and fontina

This is a lovely, chunky pizza bread – wrap wedges in foil for picnics or packed lunches. If there's any left after a day or two, eat toasted and buttered for breakfast.

Boil the potatoes in a large saucepan of salted water for 12–15 minutes until tender. Drain well and mash thoroughly. Stir in the Parmesan, salami, yeast, salt, 2 tablespoons of the oil, flour and enough water to make a soft dough.

On a lightly floured surface, knead the dough vigorously for 5 minutes, adding flour when necessary to make a smooth dough. Transfer to a baking sheet and roll out to 30 cm diameter. Cover with a clean tea towel and leave for 1½ hours, until doubled in size.

Preheat the oven to 200°C (400°F) Gas 6. Push the diced fontina into the risen dough at regular intervals and drizzle with the remaining tablespoon of oil. Bake in the oven for 30–35 minutes, until it is cooked through and golden. Let cool for 5 minutes, then slice and serve.

275 g floury potatoes, such as Maris Piper or King Edward, cubed

50 g freshly grated Parmesan cheese

75 g sliced Italian salami, cut into fine shreds

7 g sachet easyblend dried yeast

1 teaspoon table salt

3 tablespoons olive oil

900 g tipo 00 or strong white bread flour

300–450 ml tepid water

150 g fontina cheese, diced

sea salt and freshly ground black pepper

SERVES 6–8

A pizza with a distinctly Spanish flavour. As it cooks, the chorizo releases its delicious paprika juices across the pizza. I recommend using the fiery tomato sauce on this one. Serve with plenty of cold beer.

the matador

Put a pizza stone or baking sheet in the oven and preheat the oven to 200°C (400°F) Gas 6.

Roll out the dough on a lightly floured surface to 30 cm diameter and brush with 1 tablespoon of the oil. Spoon over the tomato sauce and arrange the pepper, chorizo, Manchego and olives on top.

Drizzle the pizza with the remaining oil and sprinkle with salt and plenty of black pepper. Carefully transfer to the hot pizza stone or baking sheet and cook for 20–25 minutes, until crisp and golden. Cut into wedges and serve hot.

1 recipe pizza dough (page 8)

2 tablespoons olive oil

1 recipe fiery tomato sauce (page 11)

1 red pepper, deseeded and sliced

200 g chorizo sausage, cut into slices about 2 cm thick

150 g Manchego cheese, thinly sliced

12 Spanish black olives

sea salt and freshly ground black pepper

MAKES 1

pancetta, rosemary and goats' cheese pizza

The combination of rosemary, pancetta and soft goats' cheese makes a fragrant, summery pizza. This is just as lovely served cold, making it ideal picnic food. Serve with a pile of leafy salad.

1 recipe pizza dough (page 8)

2 tablespoons olive oil

250 g soft goats' cheese

2 teaspoons coarsely chopped fresh rosemary

100 g cubed pancetta

sea salt and freshly ground black pepper

MAKES 1

Put a pizza stone or baking sheet in the oven and preheat the oven to 200°C (400°F) Gas 6.

Roll out the dough on a lightly floured surface to 30 cm diameter and brush with 1 tablespoon of the oil. Crumble over the cheese and top with the rosemary and pancetta.

Drizzle the pizza with the remaining oil and sprinkle with salt and plenty of black pepper. Carefully transfer to the hot pizza stone or baking sheet and cook for 20–25 minutes, until crisp and golden. Cut into wedges and serve warm, at room temperature, or cold.

1–2 tablespoons olive oil

500 g spicy Italian sausages

1 recipe pizza dough (page 8)

1 recipe tomato sauce (pages 10–11)

1 tablespoon raisins

1 tablespoon pine nuts

150 g mozzarella cheese,
drained and sliced

sea salt and freshly ground black pepper

1 spring onion, thinly sliced, to serve

MAKES 1

Sicilians are famous for their use
of raisins and pine nuts, one of
the many legacies of Arab
occupation in medieval times.

the sicilian

Heat 1 tablespoon of the oil in a large frying pan and cook the sausages for about 10 minutes, turning them occasionally, until nicely browned and cooked through. Remove from the heat and let cool slightly.

Put a pizza stone or baking sheet in the oven and preheat the oven to 200°C (400°F) Gas 6.

Roll out the dough on a lightly floured surface to a 25 cm square and brush with a little oil.

Cut the sausage into 2 cm thick slices. Spread the tomato sauce over the pizza base and top evenly with the sausages, raisins, pine nuts and mozzarella.

Drizzle the pizza with the remaining oil and sprinkle with salt and plenty of black pepper. Carefully transfer to the hot pizza stone or baking sheet and cook for 20–25 minutes, until crisp and golden.

Scatter the spring onion slices over the hot pizza, cut into wedges and serve.

la forketta

The invention and trademark pizza of my company, Fork – I just had to include this one. The fennel seeds and tangy orange zest really bring it to life.

Put a pizza stone or baking sheet in the oven and preheat the oven to 200°C (400°F) Gas 6.

Roll out the dough on a lightly floured surface to 30 cm diameter and brush with 1 tablespoon of the oil. Spoon over the tomato sauce and arrange the tomato slices on top. Scatter over the fennel seeds and half the orange zest. Top with the salami and olives.

Drizzle the pizza with the remaining oil and sprinkle with salt and plenty of black pepper. Carefully transfer to the hot pizza stone or baking sheet and cook for 20 minutes.

Remove from the oven and put the bocconcini over the top. Return the pizza to the oven and cook for a further 3–4 minutes, until the bocconcini have softened and started to melt, but are still keeping their shape.

Sprinkle with extra fennel seeds and the remaining orange zest. Cut into wedges and serve hot.

1 recipe pizza dough
(page 8)

2 tablespoons olive oil

1 recipe tomato sauce
(pages 10–11)

1 beef tomato,
thinly sliced

a pinch of dried fennel
seeds, plus extra to serve

grated zest of 1 orange

100 g sliced Milano
salami

12 black olives

200 g bocconcini cheese
(baby mozzarella balls)

sea salt and freshly
ground black pepper

MAKES 1

1 recipe pizza dough
(page 8)

2 tablespoons olive oil

1 recipe tomato sauce
(pages 10–11)

100 g sliced serrano or
Parma ham

3 fresh black figs,
quartered lengthways

150 g mozzarella cheese,
drained and sliced

3 sprigs of thyme

sea salt and freshly
ground black pepper

MAKES 1

Put a pizza stone or baking sheet in the oven and preheat the oven to 200°C (400°F) Gas 6.

Roll out the dough on a lightly floured surface to 30 cm diameter and brush with 1 tablespoon of the oil. Spoon over the tomato sauce and arrange the ham, fig quarters, mozzarella and thyme on top.

Drizzle the pizza with the remaining oil and sprinkle with salt and plenty of black pepper. Carefully transfer to the hot pizza stone or baking sheet and cook for 20–25 minutes until crisp and golden.

Cut into wedges and serve warm.

Salty ham and sweet figs are fabulous together. Add tomatoes and you have a dramatic blaze of colour.

serrano and fresh fig pizza

sweet pizza

3 peaches, halved and pitted

50 g butter, plus extra for buttering the dish

2 tablespoons dark rum

2 teaspoons light brown sugar

1 recipe pizza dough (page 8)

100 g milk chocolate, broken into pieces

100 ml double cream

MAKES 6

Put a pizza stone or baking sheet in the oven and preheat the oven to 200°C (400°F) Gas 6.

Butter a small ovenproof dish and sit the peaches, cut-side up, in the dish. Dot with about half of the butter. Drizzle with the rum, sprinkle with the sugar and bake for 20 minutes.

Remove from the oven and increase the oven temperature to 220°C (425°F) Gas 7.

Divide the dough into 6 and, on a lightly floured surface, roll out each piece to 10 cm diameter. Transfer the rounds to the hot pizza stone or baking sheet. Put a peach half on each round and drizzle over the juices from the dish. Bake for 15 minutes, until the base is golden.

Meanwhile, put the chocolate, cream and remaining butter in a small saucepan. Heat gently, stirring all the time, until smooth.

Transfer the pizzette to small plates and drizzle with the chocolate sauce. Serve warm.

To make the most of peaches when they are at their juiciest, cook these little pizzas in summer.

chocolate and peach pizzette

raspberry and ginger crumble

1 recipe pizza dough
(page 8)

1 tablespoon melted
butter

150 g fresh raspberries

1 piece of stem ginger
in syrup, drained and
finely chopped

50 g butter, chilled
and diced

100 g plain flour

50 g brown sugar

25 g porridge oats

vanilla ice cream,
to serve

SERVES 6

Put a pizza stone or baking sheet in the oven and preheat the oven to 200°C (400°F) Gas 6.

Roll out the dough on a lightly floured surface to 30 cm diameter and brush with the melted butter. Put the raspberries on the top and sprinkle with the ginger.

For the crumble, rub the butter into the flour until the mixture resembles coarse breadcrumbs. Stir in the sugar and oats and sprinkle the mixture over the pizza.

Carefully transfer to the hot pizza stone or baking sheet and cook for 20–25 minutes until crisp and golden. Cut into wedges and serve hot with ice cream.

Raspberries and ginger go brilliantly together. This pizza needs to be served hot from the oven, just as the raspberries have released their juices into the base.

strawberries
and cream

This is a variation on a traditional summer theme, and one which never fails to impress. Try serving it for afternoon tea on a sunny summer's day.

1 recipe pizza dough (page 8)

1 tablespoon melted butter

250 g strawberries, halved

grated zest of 1 lemon

25 g icing sugar

200 ml extra thick cream

2 tablespoons toasted flaked almonds, to serve

SERVES 6

Preheat the oven to 220°C (425°F) Gas 7.

Roll out the dough on a lightly floured surface to 33 cm diameter and brush with the melted butter.

Transfer the dough to a baking sheet. Gently push the strawberry halves into the surface of the dough at regular intervals. Sprinkle with the lemon zest and dust with icing sugar. Bake for 15 minutes, until the base is golden.

Cut into wedges and top each wedge with a dollop of extra thick cream. Scatter over the flaked almonds and serve warm.

index

A

anchovy butter and mozzarella, 37
artichokes, 22
aubergine, 20, 30
    with bresaola, rocket and parmesan, 20

B

basic pizza dough, 8
basil, 11, 15, 19, 30, 38
    mushroom with, chilli and garlic oil, 19
bresaola, aubergine with, rocket and parmesan, 20
butter, anchovy and mozzarella, 37

C

calzone, molten cheese and gremolata, 33
charred vegetable polenta pizza, 30
cheese, molten, and gremolata calzone, 33
cherry tomato, pizza, topsy turvy, 47
chicago deep pan pepperoni, 25
chilli, mushroom with basil, and garlic oil, 19
chocolate and peach pizzette, 61
classic tomato sauce, 10
courgette, 30
cream, strawberries and, 63

D

deep pan, chicago pepperoni, 25
dough:
    basic pizza, 8
    polenta, 8
    potato, 48

E

eggs, 34, 44
english breakfast pizza, 44

F

fiery tomato sauce, 11
fiorentina, 34
focaccia, tomato, 26
fontina:
    parma and fontina pizza sandwich, 43
    potato dough pizza with salami and fontina, 48
fresh fig pizza, serrano and, 58

G

garlic, mushroom with basil, and chilli oil, 19
ginger, crumble, raspberry and, 62
goats' cheese, pizza, pancetta, rosemary and, 53
gremolata, calzone, molten cheese and, 33

L

la forketta, 57

M

margherita, 15
marinara, 12
matador, the, 50
molten cheese and gremolata calzone, 33
mozzarella, anchovy butter and, 37
mushrooms, 19, 22, 44
    with basil, chilli and garlic oil, 19
mussel and pesto pizzette, 38

O

olives, 22, 50, 57

P

pancetta, rosemary and goats' cheese pizza, 53
parma ham, 22, 43, 58
    parma and fontina pizza sandwich, 43
parmesan, aubergine with bresaola, rocket and, 20
parsley, 16, 22, 33, 37
peach, pizzette, chocolate and, 61
pepper, roasted, pizza 16
pepperoni, chicago deep pan, 25
pesto, pizzette, mussel and, 38
pizzette:
    chocolate and peach, 61
    mussel and pesto, 38
polenta:
    charred vegetable polenta pizza, 30
    polenta dough, 8
potato:
    potato dough pizza with salami and fontina, 48
    potato, wafer pizza with taleggio, 29
prawn and sun-dried tomato, 41

Q

quattro stagioni, 22

R

raspberry and ginger crumble, 62
roasted pepper pizza, 16
rocket, aubergine with bresaola, and parmesan, 20
rosemary, pancetta, and goats' cheese pizza, 53

S

salami, 48, 57
    potato dough pizza with and fontina, 48
sausage, 44, 50, 54
serrano and fresh fig pizza, 58
sicilian, the, 54
spinach, 34
strawberries and cream, 63
sun-dried tomato, 26, 41
    prawn and, 41

T

taleggio, 29, 33
    wafer potato pizza with, 29
thyme, 30, 58
tomato focaccia, 26
tomato sauce, 10, 11
topsy turvy cherry tomato pizza, 47

V

vegetable, charred, polenta pizza, 30

W

wafer potato pizza with taleggio, 29